Make Me Rain

Also by Nikki Giovanni

Sacred Cows . . . and Other Edibles

Racism 101

EDITED BY NIKKI GIOVANNI

Night Comes Softly: An Anthology of Black Female Voices

Appalachian Elders: A Warm Hearth Sampler

Grand Mothers: Poems, Reminiscences, and Short Stories About the Keepers of Our Traditions

Grand Fathers: Reminiscences, Poems, Recipes, and Photos of the Keepers of Our Traditions

Shimmy Shimmy Shimmy Like My Sister Kate: Looking at the Harlem Renaissance Through Poems

FOR CHILDREN

Spin a Soft Black Song: Poems for Children

Vacation Time: Poems for Children

Knoxville, Tennessee

The Genie in the Jar

The Sun Is So Quiet

Ego-Tripping and Other Poems for Young People

The Grasshopper's Song: An Aesop's Fable Revisited

Rosa

Lincoln and Douglass: An American Friendship

Hip Hop Speaks to Children: A Celebration of Poetry with a Beat

Make Me Rain

POEMS & PROSE

NIKKI
GIOVANNI

wm

WILLIAM MORROW
An Imprint of HarperCollins*Publishers*

HarperCollins books may be purchased for educational, business, or sales promotional use. For information, please email the Special Markets Department at SPsales@harpercollins.com.

FIRST EDITION

Designed by Elina Cohen

Library of Congress Cataloging-in-Publication Data has been applied for.

ISBN 978-0-06-299528-5

20 21 22 23 24 LSC 10 9 8 7 6 5 4 3 2 1

Some folk look for the end of the Rainbow hoping to find a pot of gold; but I discovered the Rainbow in the love my Grandparents gave me in Knoxville.

CONTENTS

Make Me Rain

MAKE ME RAIN

make me rain
turn me into a snowflake

let me rest
on your tongue

make me a piece of ice
so I can cool you

let me be the cloud
that embraces you

or the quilt
that gets you dry

snuggle close
listen to me sing

on the windowsill

make me rain
on you

NO PANCAKES PLEASE

I don't like pancakes
or waffles though I will
Sometimes eat a biscuit
or a roll

I don't like French Toast
or for that matter American
Toast
or break smashing things
between two pieces

I think doughy things
are an abomination
and I would starve
to death
before I ate Kentucky
Fried Chicken
I know no white man
on Earth ever
fried chicken

I refuse to eat
a lie
But I understand
I have to do
Some things
So I hope
it is green
please Make Me Rain
So I can be a weed

that something
will find useful

Maybe a mathematician
or maybe a poet
or maybe just a star
at night
guiding
Wise Folks
to Bethlehem

A QUERY

I want to know
what song Jesus sang
while He waited on the Cross
to die

I want to know
what the soldier heard
when he didn't hear
anything more

what song did Jesus sing
that asked His Father for rest
and why did His Father send
a sword by a stranger
to let the river
flow

I'm so glad
I'm Black
because we know
there is
Salvation

YOU TALK ABOUT RAPE
(for donald trump)

They talk about Rape?
They must be kidding
Ever since the Europeans
joined the African
Slave Trade
I've been Raped

I've conceived for or against
my will
and I've delivered

We must remember Lincoln
didn't stop the Slave Trade
because it was wrong
but because there were enough
Slaves

I've delivered
I've named
I've loved

If anyone should go
into Space

It's Me

Where Space life
will treat me
like Earth life

But I will deliver

I will name
I will love
my pain will become
A Song

My hopes will live
despite trumpeting
sounds of white

supremacy

Give me left
overs
and I will create
a cuisine

Give me scraps
and I will create
a quilt

Give me life
and I will give us
all the moon
and the stars

You talk about Rape?

I talk about possibilities
I'm not the one afraid
of you

in the midnight hour
coming to lynch my sons
and force yourself on my daughters

You talk about Rape?
I'm not afraid
of any of it

I'm ready
To Go
To Mars

VOTE

It's not a hug
Nor mistletoe at Christmas

It's not a colored egg
At Easter
Nor a bunny hopping
Across the meadow

It's a Vote

Saying you are
A citizen

Though it sometimes
Is chocolate
Or sometimes vanilla
It can be a female
Or a male
It is right
Or left
I can agree
Or disagree but
And this is an important but
I am a citizen

I should be able
To vote from prison
I should be able
To vote from the battlefield
I should be able

To vote when I get a driver's license
I should be able
To vote when I can purchase a gun
I must be able
To vote
If I'm in the hospital
If I'm in the old folks' home
If I'm needing a ride
To the Polling Place

I am a citizen

I must be able to vote

Folks were lynched
Folks were shot
Folks' communities were gerrymandered
Folks who believed
In the Constitution were lied to
Burned out
Bought and sold
Because they agreed
All Men Were Created Equal

Folks vote to make us free

It's not cookies
Nor cake
But it is the icing
That is so sweet

Good for the Folks
Good for Us

AT THE IMPORTANT END

my mother at 4'11"
was never going to walk
into a room with all those
women 6'0" or so who had
on mink while she wore
cloth

they would never say
Oh Mrs. Giovanni are
you warm enough
while they ask their drivers
to grab a blanket for her

that would never happen
again

I tried to think
what my generation looked
at in the same way

Grandmother loved silver
and purchased the set
one completion at a time

I think of her eating my oatmeal
from her silver spoons

Mommy liked cashmere
but she had to have that
Mink

I would have it
no other way

I don't know what
my generation values
with the same passion

I guess when I am
in Hospice and Mike and Gloria
bring me a plate of oysters
on the half shell

if I don't
sit up
and slurp them down
immediately
you will know

Pray for me

AND SO IT COMES TO THIS

Painful words
Nasty comments
Always in groups
Never just by yourself
Teaching your sons to hate
And your daughters to fear

Waiting until night
Putting on white hoods to cover your face
Burning the Cross
You say you worship
Bombing the church Four Little Girls
Or Nine Bible Studiers
Will be in

Passing laws
No this allowed
No that

Complaining because you're poor
Complaining because you're ignorant
Sad because you're stupid
Greedy because you don't know anything else to be

Sexing your fourteen-year-old daughter
Beating your wife
Saying you are for the unborn
Unless you can be a cop
And shoot them
Or on a jury and free the men who murdered them

Or looking for a job and taking one
In Private Prisons
Where God only knows what you do to the men

Since when did Prisons become
"Private"

Killing coyotes because they howl
Killing lions if you save enough money to go to Africa
And can brag
Killing your girlfriend because she says she's
    leaving you

Looking at the world with a toothless mouth
With facial hair down to the ground
Trying to believe coal will come back

Finally having to recognize:

The only thing you have to offer
Anything . . . yourself . . . Planet Earth
Anything at all.
Is
Your white skin

How sad. How sad.

QUIET
(for Marvalene)

Quietly
you open a book
to let the sunshine in

Quiet
you hum a song
that you create
to let yourself relax

Quietly
you shed a tear
when you let a loved one
go to Heaven

Quiet
like bread rising
or your grandmother
sleeping

Quietly
when you sew
a quilt to keep warm

Quiet
as the salt melts
in the bathwater

Quietly
Quietly
Quietly

when you know
whatever else it is

you were loved

AMERICA

Strawberries
Blackberries
Blueberries
Cheese

Eggplant
Yellow squash
Boiled corn
Beets

Chocolate fudge
Cold buttermilk
Chicken wings fried
in butter

Apples
Oranges
Tangerines
Peaches

America
America
My home
Sweet
Home

BIG SISTERS

Big Sisters:
have dimples
can sing
play the piano
tap-dance
read books
talk on the phone
paint their toenails
overnight with friends

while

Little Sisters
look on
and
love

POEM
(for Samuel H. Howard)

We celebrate
and rightfully so
Those who escaped
Slavery

We are so proud
of those who ran
and those who did not
Tell
who was running

When we could not
read or write
We sang a Song
or Quilted a blanket
or showed our grand
Children
How to make stew
Because we knew

One day some of us would build
a home
a church
a school
a community
That we could celebrate

We clapped and sang
and studied

by the light
of the fire

We persevered
We made a change
We stood
Ever On The Altar

This may well be
Your life
But it is our life
Too

And we Celebrate
You

EVERYTHING BUT THE WATER

my red plaidish swimsuit
blue sandals
suntan lotion to keep me safe
potato chips
chocolate chip cookies
lemonade but no ice
Mommy's old blanket
Mrs. Frisby and the Rats of NIMH
In case I finish *Surf's Up*
the grass Daddy cut yesterday
and lots of sun
the only thing missing
is the ocean
oh well
maybe next year

I AM YOUR SWEATSHIRT

it was snowing
or maybe that was just a hard rain

it sure was cold
and all I wanted
was a fireplace
and maybe just one glass
of good red wine

I wanted the sun
to give me warmth
but the moon was so beautiful
and that Northern Star was leading my heart
astray
I thought: A pot of Pinto Beans
and a couple of corn bread muffins

I was going to shower
because I wanted to curl
my hair
my nails needed painting
and there was really just one
thing to make it all
right

You

if I could be
a sweatshirt

I could cuddle over you
and watch a good football game

sweatshirts are hard
workers

LIFE ON MARS

Maybe I ask
Stupid questions
Or make dumb
Observations

Maybe I just
Don't know what
I'm doing
But I wish
There was a softer
Voice
To answer me

If I buy
More peppermint
Or love more Leftover
Fudge
would it make
A difference

I brush my teeth
I smile
But there is always
This frown

Daddy went away
Mommy works all
The time

And nobody makes it
All Right

I think I'll run away
With the Ants
And live
On Mars

NO I.D. REQUIRED

When you grow up
Remember
I'm a train
Diesel
With wings
I can take you
Anywhere

I'm a book
You can learn
Everything

I'm fried chicken
You will never be
Hungry

I'm a quilt
To keep you warm

I'll be with
The Ancestors

So you'll have to Tweet
From your heart
But
I'll know who
Is calling

Since I only have
One
Granddaughter

SONG OF MYSELF
after Walt Whitman

if ever there were leaves of grass they would be the captured
and enslaved . . . bought and sold . . . planted and sown . . .
made to be something they were not . . . yet growing and
blossoming . . . and finding a way . . . to re-create themselves

if ever there was a song of myself . . . it was the song sung by
the old ladies . . . watching their children be snatched away . . .
watching their sons be hanged . . . watching their lovers be
whipped . . . finding a way to offer a prayer . . . to a god they
had not known

the first American poet stirred not words but love . . . pulling
fat from hog intestines . . . keeping worn pieces of cloth to
make a quilt . . . learning a language . . . to go out to the
campsite . . . to sing for that balm in Gilead . . . to rest in the
everlasting arms

Whitman heard those in the printing room . . . in the fields . . .
in the hospitals . . . in the moans of the wounded and dying

but he was not our first poet

those women who had to re-create themselves . . . and
therefore create this country . . .

they were not uneducated . . . they were not ignorant . . . they
were not afraid . . . they were simply without degrees . . . but
they were first

SOME CALL IT LOVE

I am a flower
you can put me
in your window

I don't need seed soil
only a bit of water
some sunshine
every now and then
and a kiss

I may not grow
but I'll stick
around

and wave to you
each morning

THE BLUES

Some folk think the blues
Is a song or a way
Of singing
But the blues is
History
A way of telling how
We got here
And who sent us
The blues may talk about
My man
Or my woman
Who left me
Or took my money
And is gone
But what they mean
Is I was stolen
In an African war
And ignorantly sold
Probably not
Realizing to a new world
But the Lord is Good
And gave us a song
To tell our story
We sang the blues in the cotton fields
Not to complain
About our lives but to let
Each other know
We are still here
We stirred the blues
In our stews

To give us the strength to go on
And Lord Have Mercy we used
The Blues
To give us joy to make us laugh
To teach us how to love and dance and run
Away
And much more Thank The Lord
How to stay until
The next day
The blues is our history
Our quilt
The way we fry our chickens
The way we boil our grains
To make us some really good
Something to drink
The blues is our encyclopedia
And no matter who tries to copy us
Only we know
The real meaning
Of those songs

LOVE IN ALL COLORS

If I could make a love
quilt
I'd start with peppermint
then add chocolate
in the stripes

My favorite fruit
is Blackberry
but we need a lot of sugar
on them

I guess the quilt
is not edible
but if I could eat
it
I'd have fried okra
and a couple of home fried
chicken wings
with whole garlic cloves
and ginger root
in butter

This is probably not
what Love they had
in mind
but it is what I Love

So I can either eat
or snuggle
with the love
of my Life

UNLOVED
(for Aunt Cleota)

I don't understand how folk
can purchase drugs
but not turnips
or celery roots
and I sure don't understand
why anyone would not cook
a bone two or three times

that's what makes
a quilt
again and again
and did I forget
love
why in the world would you not
want to tie love to love
to that little piece of cloth
or why wouldn't you share
love with those pieces your grandmother
or grandfather
or aunt or uncle embraced
everything has value
only sometimes
we don't know
it

my aunt Cleota gave me
a dress
from all the little pieces
of her love

how could I not
wear it with pride

I am so lucky
I will never be cold
but more
I will never be
unloved

1619 JAMESTOWN (BUT NOT ONLY)

An Answer to the *New York Times*

There may be a time line but there is no time limit to change
that does not, will not, cannot change. No matter what the
color the people or language they speak, no matter which God
is served, no matter which food is eaten or forbidden, which
clothes are worn or not, no matter the hair covered or shaved,
no matter how we look at it . . . there have been slaves. Every
civilization, or rather most, reach a point where slavery is
recognized as wrong or in some cases simply a bad idea. Or
perhaps more accurately those who used to sell slaves now
no longer have the currency or strength to control the lives
of human beings so they create a lie on a supreme court for
the same purpose. I have often wondered when I think of the
murder of Jesus what He and Simon the Cyrenian talked about
as Simon gave Jesus some relief with getting the Cross to
Calvary. We have a bit of an idea what Socrates was thinking
as he drank hemlock. In our time we know Martin Luther
King wanted to hear music at dinner "Play it beautifully
for me" before the shots took his life. And there would be
many others who were hanged, beaten to death, fought in
wars for the right or wrong side. But I have wondered, as a
person living in Virginia, how the peanut got here. We know
Europeans didn't go into communities to find west Africans.
Africans did. We know when communities recognized defeat
they were lined up and brought to shore to be sold. But don't
we also see a grandmother trying to defend her grandson and
failing, reaching to put in his hand a peanut. "Don't forget
me," she says. And he holds tightly to what will be called
America where he is sold. He plants that charge for a promise
to keep. And he stays to watch it grow. Others would escape

and think him cowardly. But he had promises to keep. Others did not understand the strength it takes to wipe spit from your hanging brother, to cradle your daughter after a rape, to lovingly put your wife into the ground. But he had promises to keep. And he kept them. Virginia is not the Peanut State. Virginia is the State of Promises. The only question is will we keep them.

IN THE EVENING

But in the evening
When the sun seeks rest
I evaporate . . . I become
Its wind

And remind us of the songs
That tell the history
Of the comfort and Love
So that the Children
May know

FOR PAT MOSS (AT THE STEGER READING 2017)

Moss doesn't bloom
But rather climbs
On Creativity
And love
To the top
Of the tree

Green and shining
With the Sun
Kissing the Robins
Wishing the Squirrels
Good Day
Or sometimes
Just parting
The leaves making
A canvas
To show Her Joy
Of Being

AFTER THE DAY

the day like me
or is that the same as
such as I
wants to wrap myself
around you
hearing C-flat
against an F-minor
humming the lullaby
to the rhythm of you reading
that silly novel
you try to complete
each night
I rest in your rest
while the day
snuggles in
and sings me
to sleep

MALCOLM X AND THE GUARDIAN

21 February 1965

It's too bad Malcolm didn't play golf. He would have easily been Number 1 without the ugly arrogance. Or maybe he should have been a comedian . . . we would all get the warmth of laughter without the shame of abuse. We know he was a singer . . . a blues man of the first order . . . because he was a truth teller. He sang a sad song of segregation and a love song of Respect for our people. I'm sure he could dance. Greg Hines has nothing on Big Red. But he couldn't dodge the bullets that took him down. He was a gentleman of the first order. Everyone felt safe in his company . . . even those he disliked . . . and those who disliked him. When they make a real movie about his life we'll see his courtship of Betty, his embracing of fatherhood, and more, his understanding of himself that he, Malcolm, was the most important person. He learned to speak for himself with us not at us. He taught us that we can change and change again seeking our better selves. We miss this great and gentle man.

Poetry is like a child in many ways: it grows and grows adding whatever is needed: teeth, longer legs, a mind that discriminates.

Or maybe it's like a thorn tree: it grows but you have to be careful how you touch it or how it touches you. It can be beautiful but it can also hurt.

We hear poetry from the moment we are conceived. Our mothers sing songs to us in the womb while they smile and anticipate. The old days were better than the new because then no one knew who we were so everyone could guess and smile and tell our mothers who we would be. No one knows what a good poem is, either. We read it or we hear it but it will be a long time before we truly understand what an impact the poem will have.

People think poetry has gotten better because the youngsters are now quoting the oldsters but it's not true. We were always young to someone else's old. Countee Cullen all but ruined Baltimore for many of us and Paul Laurence Dunbar made us stand taller when he expressed his understanding of the caged bird.

But didn't someone who is now unknown tell us she sometimes feels like a Motherless Child? Weren't those Spirituals poems of the highest order? Weren't those Spirituals the poems "that got us over? Our souls look back and wonder how we got over?" Though Langston Hughes answered that saying "I've known rivers?" my Grandmother sang "Pass Me Not, Oh Gentle Savior."

It's the nature of humans to always discover and rediscover the same thing. Aren't we all really the canary in the mine? We, sadly, might just be the donkey going blind because there is no light. Every now and then Hitler trumps along to bring hatred and some poor folks think that is a candle.

We need poetry because it brings the light of love. Everybody wants to confuse love with sex. Ask Bill Cosby about that. But love is the patience to forgive and go forth. There is no way not to like Black Americans. We try to practice love. We use the chicken feet to make a stew; we take the scraps of cloth to make the quilt. We find the song in the darkest days to say "put on your red dress, baby, 'cause we're going out tonight," understanding we may be lynched on the way home but knowing between that cotton field and that house party something wonderful has been shared.

We are poetry. And poetry is us. Those who share with us are poetry. Those who sit and eat our pig feet and chitterlins and those who come on Sunday to worship with us. There is no "Oh my goodness! The poetry is growing!" It is the soil that keeps all of us growing. So that the lemons will fall from the tree. And Beyoncé can make *Lemonade*.

FOR THERRELL SMITH

(at 100 years old: Fisk Graduate)

There was a school
built on a song
sung for the Future

Fisk

in the belief
that we go forward
with dreams
that dream not during sleep
but awake

Queen Victoria asked "Where do you come from?"
and they answered "Nashville, Ma'am."
"Why that must be a musical city."
and so it became
and The Fisk Singers returned home
to erect
Jubilee Hall
and 100 years later
the true Jubilee
was the daughter
who studied and learned
and believed in her tomorrow
and we all congratulate her
on her success of the journey

LEAVES

On a rainy day
When I'm sitting
In a tree
Looking for a friend
I hope you'll be the one
Standing at the root
Holding out your arms
To gently catch
My fall

ONE—THREE
TWO—THREE
THREE—ONES

Forty-nine years ago
on this day
my son was born

Forty-nine years later
my good friend Novella
died
and on the same day
my literary son Kwame's mother
died also

on that same day
Novella and Barbara died
they were both buried

one in New York
one in Norfolk

Everything they say
comes in threes

1 birth
2 deaths

is that three
or will we need
one more death
to make this
right

LOVE
(for Novella)

there should be a pair of ballet shoes
that embrace a wonderful actress so that she can dance
across our hearts

there should be a string
flung
no wrapped across the room
that a heart dances on it
perfectly balanced
by the love she gives
and the love we send up

there has to be something wonderful
to make for dinner
and something that is lots of fun
to talk about

Novella

that perfectly smooth heart
that always reaches out

a mother I think
doesn't ask for much more
than to see her daughter become
a beautiful caring woman
and if she is bright and giving
all the more better and

Novella

had that joy
wherever she transitioned to
we call it Heaven
there are other comforting religions
which have other words
we know
that she knows
that all will be well
from the love she gave
and the love that will continue
confidently in her name
and through her heart
to dance so smoothly
across that love

A GOOD JOB

(for Kwame's Mother)

I know we are happy
To hold them in our arms
Watching
Them squizzle
Learning
To grow
I'm not sure
What makes us happier
Watching
Them take their first step or
Watching
That first tooth come in

We certainly think
That first word should be
Mother

And what joy to
Watch
Them walk
Down the aisle
For graduation or marriage
And how fortunate are we
To see the world celebrate

The Talent

We burst with pride
At the Best Sellers

And the Prizes
But mostly I think we
Appreciate
The warmth
Of the arms of our sons
Laying us to rest
Knowing
We have done
A Good Job

THE 10TH PLANET

I'm not sure
that it is always important
that I know what people
are talking about

at my age my hearing
is weak and my memory
is weaker
but I know how to smile
and say "Yes"

I used to think
the dirt made
things grow
then I thought
it was water

But now I know
it's the evening air
and the sound of the birds
and a loving smile
from you

IN SILENCE

I wondered why
Grandmother and Grandpapa
could sit
in Silence
on the front porch

She smoked a cigarette
He didn't
Sitting on the swing
in Silence

I washed the dishes
and cleaned up
the kitchen
trying to figure
out why they sat
in Silence

Then I got to be
my own age
with my own deck
and my own person

and I understood

WINTER HOMES

My goldfish are finding
winter homes under slabs
in the pond

Mother goldfish birthed
and hid four babies
this summer

they were not eaten
by birds
or their fathers

the heater is on

it's my contribution
to mother nature

I have aired my quilts
and washed my blankets

I will cuddle
with my dog
a good book and with any luck
a cup
of Frontier Soup

finding
my winter home

BUT SOME OF US STAYED

we forget the strength
of those who stayed
behind
we sometimes don't recognize
what it took
to decide to build
a church
a school
a store to sell the yams
we picked from the ground
the tomatoes we carefully watched turn red
on the vines
to seek the okra pods
as well as to pick
our own cotton

we took pride
in our work
and lovingly encouraged
our daughters to dream

we sent them
our daughters
to school then
to college
and they stayed to help others

100 years is not
so long

when we plant
love with patience

when we find that song
that gives us strength
to go on

HAPPY MOTHER'S DAY
(from Cleo)

They say you cannot be
my real mother
because we are different
but lots of things are
different and love makes
them the same

I am lucky
to have a Mom
who drives me
and bathes me
and lets me
sometimes
snuggle in the bed

You walk on two
and I on four
but I don't need
glasses

either

WE WRITE

No matter who we are or where we find ourselves our first stories came in song. We have to remember that 10th Day on the Slave ship. On the first and second day we, the captured, were brought up to be washed with seawater and made to jump up and down to keep our muscles in some sort of shape. We could look to see the ending of the country, actually the continent, from which we came. I once had a professor who had been so very kind to me. She had helped me be accepted in the Pennsylvania School of Social Work and when that was not working for me got me accepted in the new program at Columbia University in New York called The MFA Program. I was in London for a poetry reading when her daughter called to say Louise had died. If ever there was a funeral I wanted to be present at it was hers. But the only way back to Philadelphia was the SST. I was a young poet and not having much money I tried to see how that was possible. Then I realized. It didn't matter whether or not I could afford the flight. I just needed to get someone to give me a credit card so that I could charge my flight. Someone did. And I did. The SST took off and it goes up and up. They no longer have it but it went up and up again. It was actually a rocket and there was only one seat on each side. I looked out my window as we continued to climb. The pilot finally said, "Ladies and Gentlemen, we are at sixty thousand feet. Sixty-five thousand feet. Seventy thousand feet." We could see the curve of the Earth. It was totally fascinating. My African ancestors probably did not enjoy seeing the push away but on the fifth and sixth day they could look out or over, neither they nor I know which one, and see the ending of all they knew. We know that by the 10th Day all the white people on the ship were armed because those captured would now be fighting if not for their lives, for their knowledge. We lost. Some of us were hanged. Some were thrown overboard. Some jumped. But those who understood that we were lost understood also that we had to rethink who we were or are. I always like to think it was an older woman who was put back down in the hole who understood the loss. She knew she needed to say something to her people though there is no such language as "African." So she reached into her soul and began a moan. And that moan was picked up and carried forth. By the time the ship reached what would be called America those on that ship had one thing in common: a song.

It only makes sense to me that the first word those captured understood was "SOLD." They probably thought that was their name they heard it so often. Off they were sent to various communities where they had to learn to talk to each other. The first language was a song. They sang in the evening to comfort each other and in the morning to call us all to work. These folk built homes and communities. They had skills that were put to use to plant and harvest. It is so easy to think we came from African communities with no knowledge of how to live together, which is just ridiculous. We found a way to understand we are of the same community no matter where we came from. We helped each other.

We also found a God that we learned to worship and lean on. We took that same song from the Slave ship to worship that God. And that song is what we are looking at now.

The black people who sold us and the white people who bought us never understood we were going to become a new people. We were going to build a new world. We were going to change the culinary habits of how this world worshipped. How in this world we taught our children to be strong and go forward. They thought if we were not allowed to read and write we would not appreciate who we were becoming but they were wrong. We wrote sometimes with paper and we always wrote with song. All of us passed our stories down on paper or through song. We fought for education but we also in the cool of the evening passed down our stories around the fireplace. My grandparents sat on the front porch at the end of day, after grandmother had cooked our evening meal and I had washed the dishes, and talked with our neighbors. Some call it gossip; some call it history. We talked with each other. I learned on that porch to never argue with anyone who was stupid. To never try to persuade anyone who would never agree to help. I also learned to appreciate and love the folk who came to share a secret. To say when there would be a meeting. To share what was needed to get someone up north to school or safety. If I could have been in Gee's Bend I would have learned to quilt some of the most beautiful quilts in America. I did learn to cook and not waste any part of whatever I was cooking. I did learn to listen, to be patient, and most especially I learned to cheerfully give: time, knowledge, money. What sadness it brings that we no longer sit on front porches and call to each other. What terrible sadness it is that we want the folk who sold us and the folk who purchased us to like us. We have to like ourselves. We have to love each other.

We write because we have evolved to another century. We write to be sure the words to the songs, and for those who understand, the notes to the music, get written down. We write because we are lonely and scared and we need to keep our hearts open. Black Ink, or as my student Jordan Holmes writes, Black Mail, comes to all of us because that's who we are and what we do it with. By definition. Black Mail is what we receive. And I am so glad that I do. I like those folks on the ship who created that moan that became the Spirituals that turned into Jazz and Blues and everything all the way up to Rap and whatever will come next. We who do words are doing what we do. We are not trying to get folk who are frightened of us to be calm around us. We are reminding folk who love us that this is a good thing. Black Ink should be a soup or a drink or something we can embrace with pride. Black Lives Matter. Black Ink reminds us of why.

TRAIN RIDES MATTER

I never did figure out
Why Mommy bought me
An electric train

Mostly those
Of my age
Were for boys

Maybe she wanted me
To travel
Which I did

I remember sitting
During the age of segregation
In the "colored" car
Where the Pullman Porters looked out
For my sister and me

And we didn't understand we were
Not wanted

We loved it

I remember my first trip
Alone
From Philadelphia

Back to Knoxville
To take a test for college

Two white boys
In military uniform were teasing me
About my chocolate chip cookies

That was after the trains were unsegregated

And I remember just a few years
Ago
Riding from Chicago to Seattle
And running out of good food
In Montana

But I love trains
And the men and women
Who control them

If I had my way
We'd be rid of cars
And sit on trains
And sing good songs
That Mommy taught me
And day dream that everything
Was going to be
All right
That Everything
Is going to be
All right

SPACE INSIDE MOSTLY BUT OUT

I guess I'm lucky I'm not in prison because the one thing that most people don't know about me is that I'm a space freak. If I didn't love hospitals so much I would be freakish about how that space was organized. Actually I should confess: I like my hospital room organized in a certain way. The last time I was in the hospital everybody knew I was way better when I asked to have my flowers arranged by sizing them shorter to higher. I really have a hard time when things aren't right. I have a friend who has a key to our home. She comes over sometimes when we are out of town to take a nap, which she usually does in my room. She always feels the necessity to call and tell me she has come over to rest. It finally, after five years, occurred to her that I knew when she came. My room was never the same. I can tell when someone has used my bathroom and for Heaven's sake I know when someone has stretched out in my bed. I think it's because I was always the last one to leave the house when I was a little girl. School wasn't all that interesting so I would do my chores first then go to school when school was out. Everything would be neat and I would be able to stay after school and have Sister Althea all to myself. She would talk with me and discuss books and tell me about her adventures. She was a New Yorker and she was in Cincinnati because though a lot of folks said they were Christian, only The Convent of the Transfiguration in Glendale would accept a Black American into their sisterhood. I'm sure I learned more than I can actually delineate but what I really know is that if it was supposed to be in one place I always wanted it there.

We lived in Lincoln Heights which was just beginning to be a city. I think it was a village but mostly it just was "there." We didn't have garbage collection which was fine by me because I really loved to burn the garbage. We didn't have neighbors living in the lot next door so all we had to deal with was rabbits which I liked and rats which I didn't. I think every now and then I'd see a possum but I don't remember any skunks. My sister and I shared a room. I am the baby sister so I was surprised Gary let me have the window. I could see the moon with which I fell in love and I could watch who walked up and down the side street. I recently was reading about what integration cost us. The writer was saying we lost community. I'm not so sure but we did lose Neal's Grocery Store on the corner. Neal was a Korean War veteran. On the back street was a cookie shop: two ginger snaps for a penny. I forget his name. Sis did hair on the upper street; her son Gene cut hair on the corner. When I moved to Blacksburg the one thing that surprised me was that white people didn't have hair dressing on Saturday. Black folks closed on Monday because church was Sunday and Saturday was the most important day. Women my age don't know how to swim because the pool was open for us on Saturday. The boys could swim but we couldn't because we got our hair done and no matter what the caps said water would get in and your hair would "go back" then you'd look terrible at church. It wasn't a hard choice: swim or church. Directly across the street Green's had a jukebox and folks hung out to dance. Up the opposite corner Lyle's had a grocery store. The Lyles had adopted a son named Luther and that's all I remember. Down the next corner Anderson had a drugstore and Mrs. Anderson was close to my friend Nate Green. Then you turned the corner to go to St. Simon's School which held our church and tennis courts if there is any difference. If I backed up there was a bar on the side street down from Neal's which Mommy and I would sometimes walk down to or I guess that's over to, to purchase a quart of beer. Not me. I still don't like beer to drink though in winter I don't mind cooking my ox tails in it. And that was my space. When that space was finally disrupted it was time for me to move on. Oh, did I mention The Isley Brothers lived in The Valley Homes for a while until Mrs. Isley moved them to Blue Ash and Vernon was hit by a car and she moved to Teaneck, New Jersey, and they still won all the amateur shows.

Or maybe prison would work. I'm not friendly but I am polite. I would write my favorite authors and get free copies of their books. I'd volunteer in the prison library and I'd find a corner that I'd make mine and read and dream all day. I remember when I was in the 6th or 7th grade Rose tried to bully me. She was bigger and stronger but it was one of those things that you knew the only solution was fighting. So one not too cold day she pushed me and I had to push back. I got beat up but not all that bad and since I was in an Episcopalian school I could go to my favorite nun who asked what happened. I knew she knew what happened so we just sort of sat there talking about bullying. Kids get bullied today and they shoot or stab folks. I could just sit with Sister Althea and feel loved. I had heard and sometimes seen my father hit my mother. Actually if you ask what I was doing on Saturday night about 11:00 PM. I would say listening to my father hit my mother. When I could no longer make any sense of it I was lucky enough that my Grandmother let me come live with her and Grandpapa. Now my sense of space would come through for me. I love to dust, I twice a year straightened the pantry, I learned to iron and especially to put creases in Grandpapa's undershorts: I was useful. But more, I was loved. And I loved. I'm glad I love books because whatever disappointment I would offer life, books would help me clear it up. Fortunately for me I learned to ignore my anger and hurt. I learned to create with words and though I tried real hard I could never really sing. I still can't dance. So I'm not in prison but I am still controlled by my space. I'm excited about whatever transformation there will be. If dirt makes soil better for growing Heaven must do wonderful things for the side of us we can't yet see. I'm glad I do poems. And I'm glad I had folks to support that. I'm glad, as late as it is, that I have learned to respect A Good Cry.

CHANGES

Poetically Speaking
I am not Me
And neither is Personal
So when I speak of Me it's not
Necessarily the person
It may be just a way
Of moving
The Song Along

Folks think when
They see I
Or Me
It means
I Am She
But actually I'm only finding
A voice not
For what I've
Said or done
But how
I draw
Or sing in that first person
which may only be
what I dream

Freedom of Speech
Does not include
Your right to Threaten
Me
Just as the 2nd Amendment says:
No . . . You May not Kill

There is a difference
Between
Secret and Private
Just as there are
Differences between
Desire and Want

Everything has its own
Meaning
And all
Will
Change

I COME FROM ATHLETES

There is no way that I can think of that says segregation was a good idea yet some things have to be considered. Were I in a bad mood I would point out we didn't have to be bothered with white folks. It's still strange to me that white Americans keep saying they don't want to be bothered with us: they don't want to sit next to us on buses; they want to use a different toilet; they want their own table in their own restaurants and things like that yet they came to our dances when The Blues were being featured; they rushed the stage when Nat "King" Cole was singing; they broke into our homes to take our children out to beat them to death and actually they used the most precious organ a man has, his penis, to insert forcefully into a woman or man or child. We ended up all different colors and they kept saying they didn't like us. Very strange, indeed.

Of course, the penis will soon be extinct because it has been so often misused. Like the tonsils and other useless organs one day men will wake up and it will be gone. I have no idea what will take its place but anything that is useless or misused will be eliminated. Segregation should have kept them on their side but they kept coming.

My father was from Mobile, Alabama. He was actually short, about 5'5". The lucky thing about Gus, which is what he was called, is he was smart. Fannie Mae Jones was his mother and his father was if not unknown then not known to us. What was remembered is Giovanni which is Italian and which translates to John. My father was Jones Giovanni. They were as were most Black Americans, poor. Fannie wanted her son to go to college so she had him practice basketball a lot. He came home from school and threw the ball until it was dark. Then he went inside and did his homework. He was really good at math but no one was going to give a Black boy a math scholarship in those days.

Knoxville College was a Presbyterian college looking to help poor folks and someone saw Gus shooting the basketball. They offered him a scholarship. Off he went or I guess that may be came.

Mommy was a Knoxvillian by birth. Her name is Yolande Cornelia Watson. I always thought the Yolande was because Grandpapa was a Fisk graduate and influenced by W. E. B. Du Bois. Cornelia was my great-grandmother's name so Mommy got to share it. She attended Knoxville College because that is what Grandmother and Grandpapa could afford.

Almost no woman even my age can swim because the swimming pools were segregated and they/we could only swim on Saturdays which would not do as Sunday was church. But, and this is a wonderful But, Dr. Johnson, a Black physician, thinking Black children needed someplace to play, purchased several acres of land directly across the street from my grandparents on Mulvaney Street. I'm sure Dr. Johnson didn't purchase the land because of my grandparents but luckily for us that's where it was. He had trees planted and benches and tables put there. He also put several tennis courts in Cal Johnson Park. Mommy as with many others on our side of town played tennis regularly and Mommy became quite good. Since this was segregation Blacks could not compete in the regular tournaments. They went to Wilberforce University in Ohio to play. One year Mommy got all the way to the finals where she competed against Althea Gibson. Ms. Gibson defeated Mommy but what a thrill. Mommy went on to college where she met Gus.

My guess is that he was charming. When I met him there were other issues but they fell in love and after graduation were married. This is my point. There was a photo that Mommy kept on her dresser all her life. Gus is holding a basketball and inscribed the photo: "Think I'll score?" Since you can't corrupt the innocent I was well grown before I realized he was talking dirty to her. I thought he wanted two points. Oh well.

We attended the Baptist church, Mt. Zion, with Grandmother and Grandpapa where you stood to sing and pray. When they married and had me and moved to Cincinnati we attended an AME church where you stood or sat. Since I attended an Episcopalian school we learned to kneel in church each morning before classes. As far as I can recall men knelt when they wanted to ask a woman "Will you take my name and be true to me?" Kneeling was a sign of love. I sincerely dislike that man who occupies the White House trying to take the love and faith of our athletes who are kneeling and asking the Constitution: "Will you be mine?" It will always be a sign of Hope that the answer will be "Yes." We are not the folk who divorce. We have married for life.

TRANSITIONS
(for Geralyn Drayton)

I cry thinking you
Will leave us
You cry thinking
You are going
But we all are just changing
As the leaves snuggle into the ground
And the Moles make their Winter
Homes under the trees

Seeds take a long drink
To rest and prepare for the Spring sun
And you will get ready for Heaven

All is transition and Love is Forever

We will always remember
You and You will change
And remember us
Flowers will grow
Trees will add new leaves
Birds and Chipmunks will laugh
The clouds will embrace us

Love never goes
There is only Transition

OUR OWN PATH

Sometimes we need
to try on
another person

We try on
different
shoes and socks
blouses and pants
and when we think
it might matter
better looking
underwear

We need to try
on patience
and Love
forgiveness
things of that nature

We need to remember
We are good looking
Smart Wonderful

And mostly we need
to pick and choose
Who we listen
to

so we follow
our own path

Yeah we need
to follow
our own path

DE-PLANEING

What no one understands
is when you get off a plane
you have to urinate

They are glad to see
You
You are glad
They are glad
But
You have to move
toward The Women's Room

Just one picture
for my sister she
won't believe it

You still have a place to go to

You smile

You have already taken your dollar out
for the lady who cleans

Just one more for my cousin

Yes you finally say but
I have to Pee

Will you sign just one book?

SEEDS

I wonder how people feel
waiting
I fell on the deck
trying to put the grill
up . . . though
it is only February
I can barely see
in the morning from so many pills

I have the feeling
I am waiting
Not scared
just waiting
for the next step

Transitions
that's what we are
Waiting to change

This is not a good poem
Just a question

I wonder how people feel
at this last breath
Waiting
for the Transition

But now that I've learned
to Cry

A basketball in
for the winner

Christopher Robin
leaving Pooh Bear

Me falling
on the deck indicating
and that's a grown-up word

Maybe I won't be here all that
much longer
Maybe I will
Transition

SPRING

(for Bridgette who agrees Winter is best)

Everybody likes Spring
Things grow green
flowers come up
vegetables are fresh
the evening is longer

But I like Fall
pieces of shirts
and jeans
and leftover blankets
make quilts

Jars holding
ham bones
green beans
onions
things to be
sewn together
cooked in beer

Night comes early
love gets ready
for Winter

Smiles saved
pennies put away
for Christmas

Turkeys getting fat
for Thanksgiving

Your cold feet
on me
all the important
things
that make life
so wonderful

WHEN THE MUSIC STOPPED

The man on the right ridiculed
Him
The man on the left
Believed

He had nothing else
To do
But hum a song
Which the Roman heard
Stop

"Cut him down"
and let his mother
And the Beloved Disciple
Take Him
To the Tomb

On Sunday
Of course
It was Empty

He had gone to Mars

Earth
Did not deserve
Him

WE KNEW

We knew
We who cleaned
And cooked
We who made the beds
We who cut the grass
And mined the stone
Black from dirt and skin
We knew one
Day
Our sons would read
And recite *Ut Prosim*
Our daughters would quilt
Joining *Ut Prosim*

The Hokie Nation
Would become a part
Of the Hokie Heart

We knew one day
The Hokie Nation
Would embrace us
And we would embrace
The Freedom The Hope The Promise
That *Ut Prosim* stood tall for
We knew that our lives
Would allow us to stand strong
We knew
One day we too
Would be
Virginia Tech
Yes: We knew

79

6 MAY 2018 APPROXIMATELY 9:00 P.M. OR 10:30 P.M.
(for Charles Steger)

The sun rose
in the dark
because my mother
had opened the door
so that Dr. Steger
could easily make
his way to Heaven

I know they don't drink
bourbon or scotch but
maybe a bottle of good Champagne
was popped
when he arrived

I'm sure my mother
or aunts greeted
him with a beer
a 2017 Utopia since that is the best
but others who had been
there longer
had a better bottle of Cabernet
Hundred Acre
or something in that level

A Good man
went to Good people
and surely there are those
who will celebrate
his vision and his work

But as for me
I just want to think of him
proudly
with the love in my heart
and the understanding
that when asked
I
Never
Let
Him
Down

RAISE YOUR HAND
(in favor of immigrants)

how many of you sitting
here
think some woman of color
Black Brown Yellow White
woke up this morning thinking
"Goooolly . . . I can go to the airport
and clean toilets?"

Raise your right hand

how many of you sitting here
woke up this morning thinking
"How lucky can they be
Oh Lordy I wish I could
do that"

Raise your left hand

how many of us sitting
here gave one dollar
to those women knowing
they are underpaid
and not appreciated
at all

Raise either hand

did you know if we all
gave one dollar

every time we urinated
those women might
take 100 dollars home
to feed their mother
their children
their uncle who moved in with them
their husband who will beat them

Raise any hand

how many of you
when you see those women
say "thank God
it's not me"

Raise both your motherfucking hands
and Clap

THE FIRST STUDENTS OF COLOR AT VIRGINIA TECH

(for Mary E. Brumfield)

The first woman at Virginia Tech
Was probably a washwoman who cleaned
The uniforms
And dormitories
Of the men

The first woman most likely
Fried the chicken or roasted the beef
With vegetables
While allowing others
To set the tables
And even others to not
Recognize
Her presence

The first women at Tech
Were the women who birthed
The men
But the men seemed to take that
For granted
As if they could birth themselves

There was always the question
Of who was white
And who was not
And probably there is still
Not a better answer: We are all Earthlings

The first people of color
At Virginia Tech were
People since all
People have color

Try as we do
The distinctions don't hold
Up
We are all of color
We are all colored
The only real question is:
When do we learn
To love

RAINY DAYS

I called the sun today
but she was busy
fucking behind
the gray clouds

I asked Ginney
my good friend
who makes things work
to call

But the sun wouldn't answer
her either

I opened a bottle of Champagne
and the fruit flies
surrounded the top

Lord Lord Lord

donald trump
must be president

SUBMISSION FOR THE *EBONY* COMMEMORATIVE EDITION ON BARACK OBAMA

Barack Obama

Cool . . . Casual . . .
Incredibly patient . . . Very smart . . .
Wonderful to look at . . . (Almost as well dressed as
    Steve Harvey)

Smooth . . . Wouldn't W. E. B. be proud? . . .
and Booker T. delighted? . . .
Or maybe the other way around

And someone swinging by his neck
from a fine Oak tree
while those in white pointed hats and white robes
    stood
shouting out . . . clapping . . . having a good midnight
    time
Promised to the Stars: "Don't Worry.
They think they can kill me . . . But I'm taking
    Root . . . Yeah . . .
I'm taking Root."

NTOZAKE SHANGE

As a younger sister I have always wanted a younger sister. Then I could boss her around; tell her how to wear her hair; approve or disapprove of her boyfriends.

But I also could teach her how to clean chitterlins, fry chicken, and drive a car.

With any luck I could also tell her how proud I am that she has chosen to go into the arts. That she is an exceptional writer. That people stop her in Kroger and say what *For Colored Girls Who Have Considered Suicide When the Rainbow Is Enuf* means to them while I stand on the side and smile.

I remember when that play first was performed and we all were so proud to see another young Black woman allow her creative voice to flower.

We are still proud of Paulette. We are proud she named herself and we are proud she names us.

We certainly will miss her.

THE GIFT OF NURSES

(for Melina Perdue)

Earth nurses
soil which nurses
seeds
which administer information:
how to grow

trees nurse
branches so that birds
can nurse
blue eggs
not only to celebrate
the leaves
but to create
homes for raccoons and skunks
and rabbits to nurse
the green grasses

the grasses nurse
playgrounds
for all the children
who grow to become
great nurses
who care for all of us
with compassion and warmth

nurses come from the Heavens
and we are so fortunate
that they have come
to nurse us

WHEN I COULD NO LONGER

when I could
no longer
understand
their marriage
was none of my
business
my godmother died
and left me
$50.00

Train fare
and a pound of salted cashews
to Grandmother's home

I didn't sleep well
but I woke up safe

under a quilt made by MamaDear
and sheets smelling like the mountain air
to a bowl of grits
and two pieces of bacon

of course I was happy

who wouldn't be

safe in my grandmother's
arms

I'M JUST A POET
(for Ashley Bryan)

I'm just a poet

All I have are words
And maybe a bit of hope

I wish I had Langston
Jazz and a bowl of chitterlins
well . . . admit it: cold water
corn bread

Neither of us could dance
or paint
and I seriously doubt sing

But

We have Ashley
and Love

Good for us

And all the Literate World

LADYSITTING WITH GRANDMOTHER

Rain dances nourishment
from the soil
Tears waltz love
from the heart
Sun dances a boogie
woogie while
Lorene Cary is *Ladysitting*
with her Grandmother
Question:
Who brings the beer?

LAUGHTER
(for Dr. Ford)

and when she dies
I wish she could
hurry back
to say "Yes"
I hear the laughter
I hear kavanaugh's
   laughter
I hear donald trump's
   laughter
I hear the white women in
the crowd's
   laughter
I hear the laughter
I hear it now
as I transition
I am walking
on their laughter
at me
as The Arms of The Greatest
embrace me
and hums a sweet song
as He has embraced
my sisters
as they too
heard
the laughter

QUILTS

(for Val Gray Ward)

Quilts are precious
They feed us
We sleep under them
We salute them

There is nothing
more precious
than a quilt

Some folk think
a quilt is leftover
clothes
but we know
it is made up
of loved pieces
we have saved
then sewn
together

Soup
is a quilt
wonderful vegetables
bones from a ham
other pieces added
to fresh water
garlic
and lots of love

Quilts are a flag
some folk misuse
and fly for hate
instead of the love
they were created for

America is a quilt
made up of different
folk
we came together to build
something warm
and good

The Appalachian Trail
is a quilt
showing some Americans the way
to Freedom
Freeing other Americans
as they stood helping freedom come

The Appalachian Trail
is the first
American quilt
that welcomes all
of us
as a place to rest
be safe
and find a song
to share

SISTER ALTHEA

I remember when Sister Althea first came to St. Simon's
School, where she taught the 7th or 8th grade. Everyone fell in
love with her. She was so nice and patient but she also pushed
us to learn our history and be proud of it. I finally realized I
was wasting my time coming to school during the day so I
did my chores at home and stayed caught up in my reading.
At about 2:30 I would put my school clothes on and go to
St. Simon's. It took her a minute or two before she realized I
had not been coming to school during the day but only came
when school was over so that I could have her to myself. The
Convent was about two miles from St. Simon's and she decided
to teach me to drive if I would agree to walk back home. I
was thrilled. I still don't know why she thought I should learn
at twelve years old to drive but she was right. She also didn't
seem to mind that I no longer came to classes but only to talk
with her. We became friends for life. Or maybe I should say
we are friends forever. I never get behind a wheel without
wondering what need she saw in me. But my drive continues to
push me forward.

A SHORT BIO OF NIKKI GIOVANNI

A long time ago a little girl sat in the window of the bedroom she shared with her older sister and read by finger flashlight. She looked at the stars when the battery gave way and when she got older she snuggled under her grandmother's quilts to listen all night to jazz on the radio; or at least until she fell asleep. She first fell in love with words, then they somehow seemed to fall in love with her. She got to learn history, meet people, travel everywhere; and since this is a good fairy tale, she lives happily ever after. There may be other things along the way but the words and the stars and the music are all that matter.

FERGUSON: THE MUSICAL

Starring Michael Brown with a Special Chorus of The Unarmed
August 9, 2014

PRELUDE

First: Dark stage . . . Orchestra tuning up . . . We hear voices talking . . . singing . . . laughing . . . A saxophone is blowing in the background . . . A guitar is beginning the blues . . . maybe some chicken is frying . . . a baby crying . . . beans are boiling but we don't hear that . . . we feel it

The lights come up

ACT ONE

An Officer is taking his right hand out . . . zipping his pants . . . having failed to satisfy himself he looks for a Target

Two boys . . . one much taller than the other . . . walking down the street

"Get on the sidewalk!" the Officer yells. He rubs his gun . . . there may be satisfaction yet

"We're not doing nothing" is the tenor's reply: "We're not doing nothing walking down the street . . . Clear day . . . Clear night . . . Mama's beans are hot tonight"

The young men laugh . . . Good song

Officer (bass) is unwilling to control himself . . . Satisfaction is Coming

Officer pulls out his private . . . remembers he has zipped . . .
Pulls his gun

Bang . . . Bang . . . Oooh that feels good

Tall boy is shot . . . Shorter boy hides behind a car

Officer looks right . . . sees no one

Stands over the unarmed boy

This time it feels so good

Bang Bang Bang
Bang Bang Bang

Why can't my wife do this

Tall boy's mother comes running out

"My son! My son!" She is the soprano. "You shooting my
son!"

Officer: "I was afraid" in a slow low bass tone
"He might leave me . . . I was afraid"

Cymbals ring on the Left
Bass drums in the middle
Cymbals on the right
Xylophone tingles through

Chorus: Again Again Again You killed our boys Again

Cymbals like glass break Swishing back and forth

Chorus: Not this time Not this time

Lights lower

Chorus: swings back and forth . . . Lights flash

Ferguson is afire

ACT TWO

Officer in Court: "I was afraid he'd leave me."

Judge: "I understand . . . Not Guilty."

The End

YES

spring or early fall rains
are always welcomed yet
they don't get names
like summer hurricanes or winter storms
    they don't make
the national news
they just make us happy when we walk out
to get the paper we welcome
the shower flowers embrace
the quenching thirst the robins enjoy
the softness of the ground that allows them
    to build nests
that their eggs may grow all
things matter we all say yes
to the embrace of caring and we say thank you
that you say yes
to us

VEGETABLE SOUP

I think I'm afraid
of growing old

My eyesight will fail

I won't be able to jump rope

When I turn my CD on
I won't know Miles Davis
from John Coltrane
and may not recognize Bill Evans
from Thelonious Monk

No one will want to be
around me
because I will be sad
about what I've lost

I do have a couple of potatoes
though
and a yellow onion I think
there is a turnip and maybe some
frozen peas and surely I have some garlic cloves
I hope there is a piece of ham hock
a can of tomatoes and if any luck a yellow
and a green squash always
there is a stalk or two of celery
and of course 3 or 4 carrots

Maybe I'll have
a granddaughter
who will cuddle
under the quilt our grandmother (hers and mine)
   made
who will read *Mrs. Frisby and the Rats of NIMH*
to me again
while the vegetables
she has carefully chopped
and put in chicken broth
will drift over
like sunny clouds
to tickle our noses

COOL

In the Bible
there is Revelations
In Jazz
there is Thelonious Monk
Both need John
Saint or Coltrane
to set this world
straight
or . . . no . . .
Not Straight
But Cool
Yeah, Baby, Cool

PHYSICS
(for Virginia Tech)

The question has always been:

Does light gently fall
to be embraced
by Darkness
or does the dark
pull light down

I like to think of Dark
sitting on the back porch
maybe drinking a beer
rocking back and forth
waiting for Light to come

An embrace
A smile
Darkness welcomes
the Light
folds her
tells the bats
to go to work

Evening sings
because they tell stories to each other
a fear overcomes both
but they will seek together warmth

The sun sees them
on the rocker

in the well out in Space
and sends little pieces of color
asking them to come together
for who can say No
to the sun
who only
wants you
to make a quilt
stir a stew
in exchange for sending the stars
to twinkle a tune

so the Hokie Family
can cuddle the Dark
to prepare for tomorrow's
light

IT'S JUST LOVE

It's just love

It won't sweeten your coffee
Or ice your tea

It won't grill
Your steak
Or bake your crusty
Bread

It certainly won't
Pour your olive oil
Over your shredded
Parmesan/reggiano
Lettuce

It might make you laugh

It's just love

It won't rub
Your feet or your back
It won't tousle your hair
Or paint your fingernails red
It might make you want red fingernails though
It's only love

It has no coupon
Value

Though it also does
Not expire

Just me
Just you
Yeah

Good for nothing
Love

Throw it away
When you get
Tired
Of it

THE CIRCLE

the circle goes round
without any bridges
the river comes through
with goldfish in it
our hearts jump in
we holding hands
as we float along
to other lands

THE COUNTING SONG

When I was a little girl there were things called record albums.
Some of them would have what was called a "bonus" song at
the end so you thought you were getting something extra. Sort
of like going to the grocery store and seeing a Buy One Get
One Free without realizing you could buy one for 50 percent.
I asked my class what the folk in Europe and Russia had in
common with the people enslaved in America or working in
the coal mines of Appalachia. Neither group could read or
write and a lot of effort was put into making sure they couldn't.
The folk developed folktales to help their children understand
the world and the enslaved created songs. But what was most
important to both groups was that their children could count.
If you could count you could not easily be cheated. You were
never going to get enough but you could come closer to getting
your fairer share. The enslaved and the folk made up songs and
rhymes that when the masters heard them they thought only
of the rhythm. "How cute" they would say and go on about
their business. If they understood the children were learning
to count it would have been an ugly scene. I asked my writing
class to create a counting song and since I'm supposed to be
a writer I thought it only fair that I create or try to create one
too. So here is your "bonus" poem.

THE COUNTING SONG

Give me:
1 pound of hamburger
2 fresh hen eggs
3 shakes of salt

4 pepper shots
5 ounces of tomatoes
6 pieces of bacon
that equals
1 great big smile
2 happy grandparents
3 cats just waiting
4 outdoor dogs
5 jealous neighbors
6 full tummies
and you have all the numbers you need
let's dance let's dance
let's dance

Did I forget
1 large onion
cut in 4 equal parts
2 pieces of bread toasted then pulled
into 6 equal parts

A BENCH
(for Toni Morrison)

benches aren't just pieces of furniture
sure
we find them at rest stops where birds have stopped over
and truck drivers have pulled aside
to smoke a cigarette
(no matter how bad they are for you)
and yes
in fabulous museums we find
benches decorated sometimes
with gold or bronze
and the faces of the famous
sometimes we even find benches
among the poor
which are simply logs put one across the other
or sometimes just bricks
piled and put deeply enough into the earth
to stabilize those who need comfort

but benches are actually
a metaphor
they are friends we call on sad days
they are two old ladies who bring
Duck Eggs when your Grandmother passes

they are a friend's mother
who makes a quilt for you
when she hears
you have lung cancer

and mostly they are the voice
on the other end of the phone
who says "Write"
when you are so sad at losing your mother
"Write" when you don't know where to go
"Write" when the only person who can read you
is on a Cross
"Write"
because that is your job
"Write"

BIOGRAPHY

There is a bat
In Ecuador named
Micronycteris giovanniae
Dr. Robert Baker named it
After me. He discovered it
While studying bats
And thought the big ears
Were just like me
Maybe if the bat wrote
She would be
A poet

There is a plaque
In Lincoln Heights
Where I went
To school
And a plaque
In Knoxville
Across the street from
Where my grandparents lived

I'm also lucky
To have awards and daydreams
Or is that
Daydreams
And Awards
And I'm lucky to be happy
At what I do
And how I do it

So that is this
Bio
I'm here
And if I mist
On emotional soil
A weed will
Grow

Make Me Rain

Let me be a part
Of this needed change

AND YEAH . . . THIS IS A LOVE POEM
Celebrating The Million Man March, 16 October 1995

It's not that I don't respect the brother in Baltimore or
   Washington or even
Some parts of Northern Virginia because I do . . . It's just that
   this is different

The brother who had to wake up before dawn . . . get into a car
that may or may not need a new muffler . . . a new set of spark
plugs . . . some attention to the moto . . . but who decides nonetheless
"Yes: he had to heed the call to go to Washington DC" . . . That's
the brother I want to talk about

Not at all . . . please understand . . . that I don't have a high
regard for the brother who got on the bus . . . Getting on buses
has always been a central revolutionary act of Black America . . .
Just ask Plessy or Parks . . . No . . . Getting on a bus is
an act of responsibility . . . An act of bravery . . . An act of
commitment to change

But the brother who rose from his warm bed . . . who made his
own coffee because his wife pretended to be asleep . . . because
she was scared he might not come back alive . . . and she didn't
want to let him see her fear in her eyes . . . because she knew he
needed to go . . . even if he wouldn't come back alive . . . That's
the brother I want to talk about here

I want to talk about the young brother . . . who just doesn't
understand . . . why everything he does . . . no matter how hard
he tries . . . just never seems to come out right

How if he goes bowling and gets nine pins . . . that 10th pin
would just stand there mocking the ball heading for the gutter

How if he bumps into someone on the street and says a simple
"I'm sorry" someone else jumps in his face

but if he doesn't say anything then someone says he is
uncouth . . . or how sometimes people deliberately run into
him . . . so he joined with other people like him . . . and
instead of calling it a Benevolent Society or a Brotherhood or
Rotarians . . . they call it a "Gang" . . . indicating it as a "nest"
of "vipers" and terms like that indicating things

that we find dirty and unacceptable

How when four or five white boys rape a mentally
handicapped girl they are just exercising bad judgment

but when four or five black boys rape a jogger they are all
animals and this is not for any brother who rapes any female
(they were all found innocent) and it's not for anyone who
hurts women or any other vulnerable life form

but just a word or two about black boys who don't understand
why everything they ever try to do just never seems to turn
out right

And I think "Of course" "Yes" "Why wouldn't they cry
themselves to sleep" when all they want and want to be they
already know is denied them

Why wouldn't they be afraid of the dark . . . Why wouldn't
    their hearts be

Broken when the people they
love . . . mothers . . . fathers . . . aunts . . . uncles . . .
girlfriends . . . good buddies . . . teachers . . . preachers . . .
all turn out to be untrue

And please don't tell me that basketball and baseball and
football aren't the way to go

that they should get their education

when their education will only tell them to get a talent . . .
because the people who get up . . . if not out of these cesspools
we call the inner city have something more than a high school
degree behind them

and you have to be some kind of a real fool . . . not to see . . .
that they see . . . who makes the money . . . and who doesn't

This is for the brother . . . however . . . who does . . . indeed . . .
believe . . . that there can be . . . should be . . . must be . . . a
change

It's not that I am in any way . . . unhappy . . . about the brother
who has a fine home . . . a car that is always serviced on time
. . . a job with health benefits . . . a pretty wife . . . happy smart
children . . . a dog that obeys

I'm proud and happy for him

because a people cannot do better . . . unless individuals do better

but this is about the brother who stands on street corners singing
five-part a capella harmony . . . and the brother who does break

dancing under the streetlights . . . and they took away music classes . . . so the brothers scratched then they invented CDs so the brothers rapped then they said Rap is the enemy of women

as if Yale University wasn't turning out right-wing predators who drink too much beer and don't remember what they did to whom

so this is for the brother who is simply trying to find a tone . . . to soothe his soul . . . while everyone wants to make him the reason America is way off track

And this is about the brother . . . who knowing he is a better person . . . than even he thinks he is . . . got into his car . . . in Detroit . . . or Cincinnati . . . or St. Louis . . . and headed for Washington . . . not knowing if he would be the only brother . . . to show up for the Day of Atonement . . . but knowing

if he was the only brother . . . then on this day . . . at this time . . . he would be the brother . . . to stand and say . . . to himself . . . his brothers . . . and the folks whom he loves and who love him:

I Am Sorry That Things Are Not Different

And that is a mighty powerful thing to say . . . because people want to make you . . . make miracles . . . when all any of us can do . . . is say

I Wish It Would Be Different

but this is for the brother who was willing . . . to be the only

brother . . . so if there would be laughter as he stood alone . . .
on The Mall . . . he still said

I Will Stand Because Today It Doesn't Matter If I Am Alone . . .
I need to stand and testify

and Yeah . . . this is a love poem for that brother . . . who decided
for this one point in time

I will be my better self

And we all are so very proud . . . Of You

TUPAC

September 7, 1996
He was dreaming
The stars spelled
Thug Life
They sparked
as if the Moon
was laughing
with the Earth

Someone was tickling
His toes

Wake Up Wake Up
His cousin said
We promised Aunt Afeni
We would make dinner

It's only 12:30
He answered

But we are frying
drumsticks and thighs

He turned over
Call me in an hour

No Get up now
We have to clean up

Where is my sister?

She went to the mall
I promised we
Would clean up
and cook

But I have to go to the boxing
match today

Take Me! Take Me

No—it's for the Big
Boys Not little
Mississippi cousins

He Woke up
Made Up his bed

They dusted
Washed last night's dishes
Put the electric skillet on

Aunt Afeni really likes
my chicken
You know why?

Because you can't Rap

No, Silly, Because of fresh ginger
Can I go to Las Vegas with you?

No But I'll be back
in the morning
Fry the chicken Tell Mama I love her

The car pulled up
and out He went

A clear night
The stars spelling
Thug Life

He didn't like fight
He liked words
All Eyez on Me

The fight was over

I'll get in the back
He said
Hoping to get a bit
of sleep
from Vegas back to Oakland

No No NO

You are a Star!

He didn't want to
It didn't feel
right
but to avoid
wasted words
He did

The car pulled out
So did the gun

The sparkle in the sky
called to Afeni

Thug Life

As she crossed Bay Bridge
she knew
she understood

Her son would always

Be with us

Lesane Parish Crooks
June 16, 1971 – September 13, 1996